5

VESSELS

plus

1

ATINUKE ADEREMI

Syncterface

Syncterface Media
London
www.syncterfacemedia.com

5 VESSELS PLUS 1
Six Biblical Women
and their Experience of God's Faithfulness

ISBN: 978-1-912896-15-8

Copyright © April 2021

Atinuke Aderemi

Published in the United Kingdom by

Syncterface Media

Syncterface Media, London
www.syncterfacemedia.com
info@syncterfacemedia.com

This book is printed on acid-free paper

Contents

A Word of Encouragement

As you read these short stories, my heart's desire and prayer is that the good Lord will minister to you.

The scriptures say that you should give all your worries and cares to God, for He cares about you. You also have an assurance that He who has started a good work in you is faithful to complete it.

I want to encourage you to lay your challenges, your struggles, all your cares and fears at the feet of our Father, and as you do so, I know that He will come through for you. He will perform wonders and do miraculous works that your human mind simply cannot comprehend. Do not underestimate or let go of the words and promises He has placed in your heart. He will change your name from "barren" to "fruitful woman", fill your home with the sound of joyous children and cause many to rejoice with you.

As you read this book, you will see that each vessel turned around their barren situation by going to God in prayer and receiving an answer to their petition by faith. Everyone's journey will most likely differ, but as you speak the word of God in faith and keep your gaze fixed on Him, you will surely see a manifestation of His faithfulness. Remember, God makes everything beautiful in His time.

The children that God gave to these vessels were all destined for greatness. I pray that the Lord will see you as good custodians of His gift, and as you train your children up in His ways, they will fulfil the great calling upon their lives.

God has created we women to be helpmates for our husbands. He has invested great power in us, and we must use it wisely; we should never be in a hurry to make decisions or suggestions, and we should never underestimate God and the power in His word. Our Father is mighty and faithful to bring what He said to pass even when it seems impossible.

I know that it will not always be easy, but try not to focus on what you might be going through. Fix your gaze solely on God. Take it to Him in prayer with thanksgiving in your heart and rest assured that He will never let you down!

#faithfulGod

5
VESSELS

plus

1

1

SARAH

(Genesis 12:1-3; 15:17-21; 16:1-3, 15; 17:1-22; 21:1-3)

One day the Lord appeared to Abram. He told him that he would be a father of many nations and promised to make his name great. God established a covenant with Abram and assured him that He would always be with him. Sarai loved her husband and knowing that she was barren, she gave her maid Hagar to him to give him a child, but God had other plans.

As part of this covenant, God told Abram that he and his wife Sarai would have a child and that the child would be called Isaac, the one through whom the covenant would be established. God also changed their names; Abram to Abraham and Sarai to Sarah. I believe this ushered in a new season for the couple. A new season in our lives ushers in new things; change, elevation, promotion, progression.

Both Abraham and Sarah laughed when God said they would have a child because of their ages; Abraham was 100 years old, and Sarah was 90. But then, God's ways are not our ways (2 Peter 3:8 NLT), and as promised, the aged couple were blessed with a son, a covenant child. They named him Isaac, meaning laughter.

God can use anyone regardless of who they are, where they come from or how old they are. He turns circumstances and situations around to showcase His power and manifest His glory. God does this through His children to help others grow in confidence and build faith in His word.

Lessons

1.
Sarah loved her husband and submitted to him

2.
She was beautiful and could influence her husband

3.
She was quick to make decisions, and harsh and jealous when things did not go her way.
(We should learn to stay calm when making decisions and not blame others when things are not going our way)

4.
She initially did not have faith that she could bear a child, but her confidence grew as she believed the promise of God

5.
She witnessed the manifestation of God's word in the birth of Isaac

6.
She was the mother of many nations

Prayer

We Heavenly Father, help me not to make decisions in haste. Help me make the right decisions and give the right advice. I pray that I will have my eyes fixed on You and that my trust will always be in You. Please help my faith in You to stand firm, and give me the grace to wait patiently for the manifestation of Your word.

Father, give me a listening ear so that I can hear Your voice at all times Lord. Use me for Your glory and showcase Your power through my life. Let me always find favour with You. Thank you, Father, for Your love and making me a custodian of Your children who You have blessed with great destinies. I will bless your name at all times, in Jesus' name. Amen

.

REFLECTIONS

2

HANNAH

(1 Samuel 1)

*H*annah was married to Elkanah. She was his second wife. Elkanah loved Hannah a lot, and each time they went to Shiloh, he would give her a double portion of the sacrifice because Hannah was barren. Peninnah, Elkanah's first wife, regularly taunted Hannah because of her infertility. Understandably, Hannah was sad; she found herself weeping a lot and eating very little.

Finally, Hannah could take it no more. The scriptures recall that one day after eating a sacrificial meal at Shiloh with the rest of the family, Hannah got up and went to spend time alone with God in prayer. Hannah was in so much pain that she could not even pray aloud. As she prayed silently, Hannah made a vow to God: She would give her child to serve the Lord if the Lord granted her request for a child.

Eli, the Priest, saw her and thought she was drunk. Hannah explained that she was not drunk but depressed and that she was simply pouring out her heart to God. Eli then told Hannah to go in peace and asked God to grant her request. Hannah left believing, and the rest is history. She was blessed with a son named Samuel, and she fulfilled her vow by taking him to the Lord's house in Shiloh.

There are times when we go through challenges and trials that are so painful, times when even though our lips are moving, our prayer is silent. Be assured, God hears!

Lessons

1.
Hannah was a woman of faith

2.
She was persistent in the place of prayer; she never gave up

3.
She prayed silently, but the Lord heard

4.
She was committed to serving God

5.
She fulfilled her vow to God

Prayer

Father, I thank You for who You are to me. Help me grow in faith, knowing that your ears are attentive to my cry as I pour my heart out to You like water before Your throne. In all the challenges and trials I face, please help me see myself as the fruitful vessel You love so dearly.

Father, give me the strength and grace to wait on You and fulfil the vows I make. Help me to learn how to delight myself in Your presence and not be consumed with my needs. Father, I thank you for the manifestation of Your promises. Thank You for answered prayers, in Jesus' name. Amen

.

REFLECTIONS

....
....
....
....
....
....
....
....
....
....
....
....
....
....
....
....
....
....

3

ELIZABETH

(Luke 1:8-37)

Zachariah was a Priest, and Mary's cousin (mother of Jesus). Elizabeth was his wife. Elizabeth was considered to be barren as she did not have any children, and both she and Zachariah were old.

One day an angel called Gabriel appeared to Zachariah in the temple and told him that God had heard the couple's prayer. Zachariah and Elizabeth would have a child, and they would name him John. Angel Gabriel told him how glad and happy they and many others would be when their child was born! John would be great in the Lord's sight. He must not drink any wine or strong drink. From his very birth, he would be filled with the Holy Spirit. He would bring back many of the people of Israel to the Lord their God. He would go ahead of the Lord, strong and mighty like the prophet Elijah to the way of thinking of the righteous; he would get the Lord's people ready for him.

Once Elizabeth found out she was pregnant, she stayed away and said, "He has taken away my public disgrace!" Angel Gabriel, who had earlier told

Zachariah they would have a child then appeared to Mary and said to her that she would have a child, the Son of God. He told Mary that Elizabeth was six months pregnant, even though she was very old. There is nothing that God cannot do!

In Elizabeth's case, we clearly see that God does not work with man's timing. He is the sovereign God. Man worries about what people say, but God takes away our shame and opens our eyes to see that nothing is impossible with Him.

Lessons

1.
Elizabeth was barren, but God turned this around

2.
She found favour with God and was blessed with a child in her old age

3.
She obeyed every instruction she was given in raising her son, John the Baptist. And as promised, John was a blessing to all

4.
She had her shame taken away by God

5.
She had a testimony that once again proves that there is nothing impossible with God

Prayer

Father, I pray that You will take away my shame. Help me to work in Your time and season and not the world's. May I find favour in your sight O Lord. Father, I pray that You will speak to me concerning the child/children You will bless us with.

Help me always to believe Your word and obey your instructions regarding our child/children, and may they bring joy to everyone who comes their way. May our children be used for signs and wonders, and I pray that they will fulfil their purpose and destiny. Lord, I thank You, for who You are to us. Amen

.

REFLECTIONS

....
....
....
....
....
....
....
....
....
....
....
....
....
....
....
....
....

4

RACHEL

(Genesis 30:1-24)

*R*achel was Jacob's second wife, and she was also barren. After a wedding night mix-up, Jacob had married Leah, Rachel's sister. Rachel became jealous of her sister because, unlike her, Leah was blessed with children. When she could take it no more, Rachel demanded that Jacob give her children and that she would die if he didn't. Her words angered Jacob, and he replied, "Am I in the place of God, who has kept you from having children?" So, thinking she could have children through surrogacy, Rachel gave her maid Bilhah to Jacob.

Bilhah had two children for Jacob, but Rachel's heart desire was to have a child of her own. And so the scriptures record in verse 22 that God remembered Rachel; He listened to her and opened her womb. Rachel cried to God; He heard her cries, took away her barrenness and blessed her with two children, Joseph and Benjamin.

Whatever you may be going through in life, never look to man for a solution. You must cultivate a personal relationship with God.

Lessons

1.

Do not compete over things that are out of your control

2.

Do not be jealous or envious of others and their achievements. Instead, rejoice with them while trusting God to turn your situation around

3.

Do not look to man to make things happen for you. Remember, Jehovah is the only Way Maker, the One who makes all things possible

4.

Do not stop praying.
Just like Rachel, the Lord will remember you

Prayer

Father, I look to You for my help comes from You, the Most High and Excellent One, the One who makes the impossible possible. Father, help me stand on Your firm foundation for my life, which is your word. Please help me be a joyful person, rejoicing in Your goodness in my life and the lives of others.

Father harken to my cry and remember me, O Lord. Take away my shame and cause men to see Your glory. Thank You for making our children great. Thank you, Father, for making us vessels that showcase Your power, in Jesus' name. Amen

REFLECTIONS

....

....

....

....

....

....

....

....

....

....

....

....

....

....

....

....

....

....

....

5

REBEKAH

(Genesis 25:21-34, Genesis 27:1-29)

*R*ebekah was Isaac's wife, and just like the women mentioned in the previous chapters, she was barren. From the bible, we read that Isaac prayed, and God answered by blessing him and Rebekah with a set of twins, Esau and Jacob.

Rebekah had a rough pregnancy and feeling that something was not quite right, she inquired of the Lord. God told her that she was carrying two nations inside her; one nation would be stronger than the other, and that the older would serve the younger.

Rebekah favoured Jacob while Isaac preferred Esau. So, one day after listening in on a conversation that her husband had with Esau, Rebekah hatched a plan. By getting Jacob to pretend that he was Esau, she was able to deceive Isaac. And so it was that Jacob received the blessing.

Rebekah was determined, and she was daring. She was also a woman of faith, and she witnessed the manifestation of God's promises.

Lessons

1.
Rebekah was barren. Isaac prayed on her behalf, and God answered; He blessed the couple with twins

2.
She was a woman of faith

3.
She was kind, generous and bold

4.
She practised favouritism and was manipulative.
(It is always better to do things the God-way than to try and manipulate your way out of or into a situation)

Prayer

Father, may I have the heart to serve, and be a blessing to those I come into contact with. Please teach me to treat everyone fairly. Father may Your grace be sufficient for me to stand on Your word and promises for my life, and may my ways be pleasing to You. Help me, Heavenly Father, to live a life free from sin. I pray that Your word will be a light to my feet, and it will guide me to make the right decisions.

Father, hear my cry and grant my heart's desire for beautiful, healthy children; children who will fulfil their purpose and whose ways will be pleasing to You. Thank you, Father, for answered prayers, in Jesus' name. Amen

REFLECTIONS

....
....
....
....
....
....
....
....
....
....
....
....
....
....
....
....
....
....
....

6

THE SHUNAMMITE WOMAN

(2 Kings 4:8-37)

The Shunammite woman was married, wealthy, and an influential person in the village of Shunem. However, she did not have a child. She had a heart of compassion and asked her husband to build a guest room for Prophet Elisha, who often travelled through the town.

Elisha asked Gehazi his servant to find out how they could repay the Shunammite woman for her hospitality, and Gehazi told Elisha that her husband was old and she had no child. So, Elisha called the lady and said she would give birth to a child within a year. Within a year, she had a son.

A few years later, her son fell ill and died. She laid her dead son on Elisha's bed and immediately went looking for Elisha. He came, prayed for her child, and the child came back to life.

The Lord will always raise destiny helpers for us, so being sensitive to the needs of those around us is paramount. We should also be willing to help and honour men of God.

Lessons

1.
The Shunammite woman was a woman of influence

2.
She was kind and hospitable

3.
She was barren

4.
She had faith and did not fear

5.
She was discerning

6.
She was rewarded for her compassion and kindness.
God blessed her with a son.
He also brought her son back from the dead

Prayer

Father, may I have the heart to serve, and be a blessing to those I come into contact with. Please teach me to treat everyone fairly. Father may Your grace be sufficient for me to stand on Your word and promises for my life, and may my ways be pleasing to You. Help me, Heavenly Father, to live a life free from sin. I pray that Your word will be a light to my feet, and it will guide me to make the right decisions.

Father, hear my cry and grant my heart's desire for beautiful, healthy children; children who will fulfil their purpose and whose ways will be pleasing to You. Thank you, Father, for answered prayers, in Jesus' name. Amen

REFLECTIONS

....

....

....

....

....

....

....

....

....

....

....

....

....

....

....

....

....

The Final Word

Each of the children God blessed these women with were children of great destiny, children with great assignments. God is never late to answer; He is working it all out for good, and He will bless you with outstanding children. The question is, "Are you ready for this great assignment?"

All I can say is that you should go to God in prayer and ask for grace, wisdom, patience and everything required to train your children and prepare them for their assignment.

5
VESSELS
plus
1

The Salvation Prayer

Dear Father,
thank You for the price You paid.
Thank You for dying on the cross for me.
Please forgive all my sins.
I accept You into my life as my Lord and Saviour.
May I live my life to please You
and follow after You
all the days of my life.
Amen

Shoshana Fellowship

Shoshana Fellowship is a ministry birthed to pray for and with couples trusting God for children and women who are hurting.

We come together to pray twice a month and have "Word Works" once a month, where we talk on different topics to encourage and learn from each other. As we pray and have "Word Works", we build our faith and intimacy with God.

Our desire is two-fold; to see couples blessed with beautiful children and to see women healed and whole; confident in themselves and their God-given identity.

Our confidence is that couples will testify of God's faithfulness.

SHOSHANA

shoshanafellowship.com